Journey through

N O R W A Y

Photos by

Max Galli

Text by

Ernst-Otto Luthardt

Stürtz

CONTENTS

Page 1:
The old Hanseatic quarter of Bryggen in Bergen, rebuilt after the great fire of 1702.

Previous page:
Fishing for salmon in the Åfjord near Trondheim. Anglers can indulge their passion for free in the fjords and in the sea, but fishing in Norway's many lakes and rivers requires a state permit.

Below:
Aker Brygge in Oslo is not just a good place to shop but also popular for its humming outdoor pubs and cafés.

Page 10/11:
Urnes on the Lustrafjord has Norway's oldest stave church from the 11th century.

Page 12/13:
The little fishing village of Reine is the main town on the Lofoten island of Moskenesøy.

Right:
A cable car glides up the 400 metres (1,312 feet) of the Storsteinen from Tromsø, Norway's most northern university town bustling with young students. The view of the Balsfjord from the top of Tromsø's local mountain is breathtaking.

It is the year 793. Lindisfarne Monastery off the northeast coast of England is about to suffer the earliest commando attack in recent European history. Narrow boats with horizontal sails and fearsome dragon heads at their stern steam towards the shore, their occupants quick with the sword and dagger. The monastery is destroyed, plundered and its inhabitants murdered, leaving the Christian West scarred forever by the bloody deeds of the ruthless Norsemen. This first spectacular coup by the Vikings, ferocious seafarers who took their name from the "viken" or coastal bays of their homeland, was to be the first of many. Their operations rapidly extended to include new territories; no ocean was too big, no booty too far away for the bearded warriors. Civilisations from Europe to Asia Minor learned to quake in fear when they heard the word "Viking" ...

This contact with the western world wasn't without consequence for the Vikings themselves. They soon realised that sacking and pillaging were only one way of seizing another's assets – and not always the most profitable at that. Trade, too, had its advantages, as did the commandeering of larger stretches of land as opposed to spontaneous raids. The Northmen soon began to settle in England, Scotland and Ireland, in the Shetlands and Orkneys and also in the part of France which today still bears their name – Normandy. They not only discovered and colonised Iceland but – long before Christopher Columbus – also parts of America (now Newfoundland).

FROM CHRISTIAN TO KING

The Vikings imported goods, slaves and also Christianity to Norway, the latter violently opposed by much of the indigenous population. One of Norway's minor kings, however, a certain Harald Hårfagri (Fair-

Hair) from the Oslofjord, saw the new religion as a chance to spiral to political heights. A Christianity based on the sovereignty of one god was the perfect legitimisation Harald needed to justify the existence of a single ruler – namely himself. He subsequently elected himself head of the empire after defeating his adversaries, the tribal kings of southwest Norway, in c. 885.

Norway's conversion to Christianity was slow, often bloody – and cunningly undermined by hangers-on of the older pagan rites. While the Christians were building their stone churches in the developing towns and cities, the rural population manifested their belief in Viking tradition by erecting stave churches of wood. Most of what were once over 800 stave churches later burned down and many were carted off to open-air museums, but around 25 of them have remained in situ, perhaps the most famous being the church of Borgund (Møre og Romsdal). Dragons with gaping mouths breathe down from the gables onto would-be worshippers, the entrance guarded by a high "ghost threshold". The main supports of the building are the upright timber posts or staves at its corners, hence the term "stave church", a remnant of ancient Viking architecture which has survived intact to this very day.

THE RISE AND FALL OF NORWAY

In c. 1260 the Norwegian empire was at its most expansive. Just a century later 400 years of (forced) union with Denmark began, culminating in the loss of Norway's budding national identity. Once mighty, Norway was now a minor under the protection of various guardians, the dreaded Danes being usurped by the Swedes as Norway's keepers in 1814 following the Treaty of Kiel and the proclamation of the first constitution.

THE 20TH CENTURY

Norway finally became an independent state in 1915, too late to stop the flood of emigrants to America which had begun in the 19th century. Managing to remain neutral during the First World War, in World War II the country was occupied by the Germans. This was Germany's second historic invasion of Norway, the first being in 1250 when a colony of German trade magnates and craftsmen set up shop in the heart of Bergen and as a state within a state had a firm grip on national economy. The third invasion started in the 1970s and shows no signs of abating. Particularly during the German summer holidays the steel bellies of Norway's fleet of ferries spew out a never-ending stream of cars and caravans which clog up the roads of the mainland for hours at a time.

One of the main reasons for joining the mass exodus is the absolutely fantastic scenery. Norway's modern infrastructure is also readily accepted, although the average holidaymaker fails to realise that this has only been established in the recent past with a lot of money and effort. Traditional occupations, such as shipbuilding and shipping, fishing and timber, now coexist alongside other branches of trade which include heavy industry, titanium, zinc and copper mining, light industry, petrochemicals and diverse high-tech enterprises of various designations.

The old Viking mentality is perhaps best sustained by the oil platforms jutting out of the North Sea. The Norse nose for discovery, a great attribute common to explorers and scientists from Fridtjof Nansen and Roald Amundsen to Thor Heyerdahl, has sniffed out significant reserves of gas and oil in the waters off its shores. Today these are the mainstays of the Norwegian economy and the reason why what was once such a poor country now has the third-highest per capita income in Europe.

THE NORWEGIAN SYSTEM OF MEASUREMENT

Although not quite as badly off as the Finns – who are also isolated by way of language – the Norwegians do suffer from the rather remote geography of their homeland. Their method of edging nearer to the centre of Europe from its northernmost extreme by cunning calculation, however, has in the past pulled the wool over many pairs of eyes. The Norwegians claim that the capital of Oslo lies exactly halfway between Italy's northern boundaries and the North Cape (Nordkap), thus putting all Central European measurements of distance and the time it takes to travel them by car in exaggeratedly relative terms. First-time travellers to Norway disembarking from the ferry in Kristiansand, Larvik or Oslo and optimistically setting off

on the first (allegedly short) leg of their journey discover – after the first 60 miles or so – that here you can consider yourself lucky if you can cover even this comparatively short distance within two hours – without a break.

It's exactly 1,752 kilometres (1,089 miles) from Cape Lindesnes in the south to the North Cape – as the crow flies. Where Finland has nice, straight roads which would make this distance bearable, the thorough-fares of Norway are long and winding, with mountains, fjords and lakes constantly obstructing your path. One fourth of Norway is over 1,000 metres (3,000 feet) high, with two thirds alone over 300 metres (980 feet), resulting in a multitude of massif elevations and glacial obstacles which have to be driven round – not to mention the hundreds of fjords cutting into Norway's system of highways and byways. Ferries, of which there are about 200, are absolutely indispensable. Good job the Norwegians are so good at building tunnels – or journeys would be even longer.

NORWAY'S BEATING HEART – THE SOUTH

One third of the population live in and around Oslo. Despite this, Norway's great metropolis doesn't even total half a million inhabitants. The most impressive approach to Oslo is along the Oslofjord which like a long umbilical cord links the capital to the North Sea. Many visitors think they've seen enough after taking in the spectacular scenery upon arrival and hurry on to other destinations inland, maybe stopping off briefly at the Viking Museum and to shop at Aker Brygge – or at a pinch to marvel at the Vigeland sculptures dotted about the Frognerparken. Although impressive in its forest setting, Oslo seems destined to remain a mere prelude to the breathtaking natural spectacle which lies further afield.

The Norwegians themselves seem to like the south coast, the Sørlandet, better than their German guests. Here they can bask on Norway's most beautiful sandy beaches and

The Lyngenfjord in Troms
in northern Norway.
Under 150,000 populate   the province's 30,000 km²   islands linked to the
(11,580 square miles),   mainland and each
half of whom live on the   other by ferry.

enjoy the highest summer sea temperatures of 17–18°C in the country. In bright sun the pale sand lazily battles to outshine the white wooden houses perched along the shoreline. And if you take the time you'll discover that the south coast has more to offer than seashore and log cabins. With Kristiansand as a base, the towns and villages along the coast are well worth exploring. The old town centres of Flekkefjord, Lillesand, Mandal, Arendal, Frederikstad and Tønsberg, for example, still have all the charm of an ancient maritime port. In Åsgårdstrand you can tread in the footsteps of the painter Edvard Munch and in Grimstad or Venstøp in those of writer Henrik Ibsen.

The archipelago of the south is particularly captivating; the island of Merdø even has a good museum devoted to this unique landscape. Undoubtedly the most attractive route from the coast to inland Haukeligrend just south of the legendary Hardangervidda plateau has been forged over millions of years by the Otra River carving its way up the Setesdal. This is romantic Norway at its best, complete with monumental mountains, dense forest, wild, raging rivers, lonely villages upholding ancient crafts and customs and fantastic ski resorts.

THE LONELINESS OF THE MOUNTAINS, THE HOMELINESS OF THE VALLEYS – THE EAST

According to statistics, around 4.27 million people populate the 325,000 square kilometres (ca. 125,480 square miles) of Norway, which makes around 13 per square kilometre. This is, of course, pure speculation; over three quarters of the country's residents are squeezed into a narrow strip of coastline about a dozen kilometres wide. An ancient seafaring people like the Norwegians only seem happy close to the sea or its inland equivalents, the fjords and lakes, fishing having played an important role in their lives since the arrival of the first settlers.

This almost sacred maritime existence was renounced only if an alternative lifestyle promised richer yields. The abundant supply of silver and copper in mining towns Kongsberg and Røros, for example, was reason enough to entice the Norwegians inland. By 1957, however, after 400 years of

service, the pits had been milked dry; the only people to venture underground at Kongens Gruve now are the tourists. Røros has undergone a similar fate yet has managed to hold on to its wooden, reddish brown miners' cottages, an attractive legacy from the days of the copper mine now protected by UNESCO.

If you don't take the direct route to Lillehammer from Oslo you could well find yourself in the wonderful mountain resort of Lom where your journey can take you in three different directions, south, west and east, which in Norway is pretty rare. Jotunheimen, the "land of the giants", lies south of this crossroads. The highest mountain pass in Norway curves up to 1,430 metres (4,691 feet) and into a bizarre world of wild peaks and endless plateaux, of frozen glaciers and gushing, icy lakes and waterfalls. This mammoth landscape is girded by monumental rocky summits and to the west is enclosed by the largest glacier in Europe, the Jostedalsbreen. Elevations topping 7,000 feet are also common to the Hornunger range to the southwest and the Dovrefjell to the northeast, where reindeer and musk oxen roam wild. To reach Dovrefjell from Jotunheimen you have to cross the Gudbrandsdal; of the three great valleys which characterise eastern Norway – Valdes and Hallingsdal being the other two – this is undoubtedly the most famous. This is partly thanks to the infamous character who gave the valley its name, Dale-Gudbrand, who in his day strongly resisted King – and later Saint – Olav's endeavours to convert the Norwegians to Christianity. These valleys – like the pinnacles which enclose them – also have extraordinary proportions. The Gudbrandsdal is over 200 kilometres (120 miles) long, running into Lillehammer in the south. The ancient route through the mountains is sprinkled with farms and settlements through which Norwegian kings once passed on their way to coronations in Trondheim. The Gudbrandsdal is now inundated with an entourage of visitors trying to recapture the idyll of traditional rural life in magnificent surroundings.

Lillehammer itself became famous in 1994 when it was beamed onto TV screens across the globe for the Winter Olympics. The town today is much quieter and sleepier, its current number one attraction possibly the best open-air museum in the country, Maihaugen.

FJORDLAND AND MORE – THE WEST

Hemmed in by precipitous walls of rock which are both oppressive and curiously uplifting are the steep, sheer roads of Fjordland with bends which almost defy comparison with the hairpin, making even the best of vehicles and drivers perspire with concentration. The best-known of these serpentines are the Ørneveien, the Eagle's Highway, and the Trollstigen or Troll's Ladder. Where the mere automobile struggles to master vertiginous curves and elevations, the railway glides almost effortlessly onwards and upwards. Until the 1960s the Bergensbanen, built at the beginning of the 20th century in an operation which greatly tested the prowess of man and machine, was the only direct connection between the east (Oslo) and the west (Bergen) – apart from the plane – which was serviceable all year round. Long after the passes have become inaccessible, the train snakes through the endless snowy wastes of the Hardangervidda, Europe's largest mountain plateau, like a long black serpent. One stretch along the line is particularly challenging; between Flåm and the Myrdal junction the Bergensbanen has to negotiate a 900-metre (2,950-foot) change in altitude, 20 kilometres (12 miles) of track, a gradient of up to 5.5%, giddy ravines, tunnels, wooden supports shoring up the mountain and an interim stop at the Kjosfossen Falls which plummet 200 metres (656 feet) down into the valley.

An ideal place from whence to explore the west from the coast is Bergen, made a royal seat in 1217. The city is not only large by Norwegian standards but also extremely appealing. Enclosed by water and high mountains and blessed with the mild climate of the Golf Stream, Bergen's wooden houses and lush, colourful gardens ooze all the charm of its imperial and Hanseatic past. The gabled town residences of German merchants and traders from the 14th to 16th centuries are among the most popular sights in the city. Ålesund to the north is very different; it's not only much smaller (where Bergen has 215,000 inhabitants, Ålesund has just 35,000) but also much younger. Old Bergen goes back to the Middle Ages; after a terrible fire in 1904 Ålesund had to begin anew. The result is a playful melange of Art Nouveau straddled across three marine islands with plenty to amuse and enchant its visitors.

Speaking of the sea, even the most sober of geographers go into raptures about the unique marriage of land and sea along Norway's west coast. This union has proved so passionate, with countless coves and fjords the fruit of its loins, that the coast is twelve times longer than it would be if it ran in a straight line. The best way of admiring this coupling of the elements without losing too much time on your journey north is to drive along the Atlantic Highway between Vevang and Kårvåg near Kristiansund. Clever engineers and highway contractors have managed to join rocky islets and islands with 8 kilometres (5 miles) of dams and bridges. With a storm blowing and the windscreen wipers going hell for leather, it's like being tossed about in a four-wheel submarine.

And what about those famous fjords? With so many it's almost impossible to choose. Ones which shouldn't be missed are the Hardangerfjord when the fruit trees are in blossom and the Nærøyfjord, an offshoot of the 180 kilometre- (111mile-) long Sognefjord and the narrowest in Europe. As no road runs along its entire length the perpendicular mountain peaks towering up 1,000 metres (3,280 feet) from the water have to be appreciated by boat. Another of the Sognefjord's offspring is the Fjærlandsfjord which almost embraces the southernmost tip of the Jostedalsbreen glacier. And – last but not least – Norway's most popular picture postcard motif is a must; the Geirangerfjord is balm for the soul.

BENEATH THE MIDNIGHT SUN

Like all Scandinavians the Norwegians' pace and temperament is governed by the seasons. In the long summer nights they are merry and outgoing, in the darkness of winter quiet and reserved. The midnight sun north of the Arctic Circle creates days which never seem to end and causes havoc with the mind, with body clocks fruitlessly awaiting the fall of night to trigger sleep.

Those who venture into the barren wastes of the north are usually in search of the Absolute: the North Cape, where the midnight sun shines from the middle of May to the end of July. The object of their desire lies on an island. From the main town of Honningsvåg it's a long 30 kilometres (18 miles) plus through monotonous, bleak scenery to

the cape. The most northerly point of our European continent has become something of a place of pilgrimage. Critics complain of it being more commerce than countryside, with the view only spectacular in good weather; whereas this is not omnipresent the tacky souvenir shops are. And a good deal of imagination is called for to realise that although this may be the final spit of land on our continent, it's not the end of Norway. Far out in the North Sea the Svalbard archipelago, better known for its main island Spitsbergen, claims this title, with the North Pole a "mere" 1,000 kilometres (620 miles) further on.

THE LAND OF THE SAMI

The exact number is unknown but it's thought that there are around 40,000 to 60,000 members of the Sami population still living in the north of Norway. Originally from southern Finland, this mysterious tribe were driven to the inhospitable north where they began to eke out an existence herding and breeding reindeer. Their ancient hunting and grazing lands have long been dissected by national boundaries, with the free nomads of the north finding themselves citizens of Russia, Finland, Sweden and mostly Norway practically overnight. The greatest changes to Sami culture and society, however, are most evident when you see pictures of nattily dressed farmers herding their flocks by helicopter in the summer and motorised sleigh in the winter.

If you want to learn more about the past and present of the Norwegian Sami (who have had their own "parliament" since 1989) and perhaps pick up some original items of handicraft for friends at home, then Karasjok is a good place to head for. If you're lucky enough to visit a Sami home, then you'll really find out what day-to-day life is like, what makes them tick – and what they like to eat. You may find the dried reindeer ham requires a lot of energetic and patient chewing; the tender goulash with cranberries is a much easier morsel to swallow. Even the salmon seems fresher and tastier than any other you've ever eaten.

THE MOST BEAUTIFUL SEA JOURNEY IN THE WORLD

Tourist agencies are pretty good at superlatives. The Norwegians, usually modest in their choice of words, are no exception when it comes to the 11 days and over 2,500 nautical miles spent aboard one of the coastal cruisers of the Hurtigrute, unashamedly lauding it as being "the most beautiful sea journey in the world". Those who have put the trip from Bergen to Kirkenes to the test heartily agree – which is saying something when you consider just how many different ways there are of travelling to, from, around and through Norway by water.

The first postal ship to undertake the summer round of the cities and remote communities along Norway's jagged northwest coast was the Vesteraalen in 1893. Back then the ship's freight consisted of the mail, parcel post, a handful of locals and various goods – including animals; today most of the passengers are tourists looking for (safe) adventure on the waves and a certain degree of comfort in return for the (not inconsiderable) cost of transportation.

All things said, this unusual journey is still an experience. You see most during the (short) summer, of course, where night turns into day. As a basic rule of thumb, the larger the community (there are 36 harbours along the route) and the larger the freight, the more time there is for shore leave and sightseeing. Trondheim is a safe bet, with its splendid historical buildings and magnificent Nidaros Cathedral. Or Tromsø, with its student flair, or Hammerfest, the northernmost town in the world.

The one thing you won't see along the Hurtigrute is the North Pole, although if you believe the reports this doesn't stop the odd tourist looking for it – with or without a pair of binoculars.

Page 24/25:
The Hurtigrute coastal cruiser Narvik, launched in 1982, travelling between Hammerfest and Skjervøy.

Page 26/27:
Near Nesseby in Finnmark. Like Karasjok, Kautokeino, Polmak and Tana the little community is primarily inhabited by Sami.

THE SOUTH – DEEP

The island of Vågasøy just off the coast of Fjordland. Lighthouses such as Kråkenes fyr guide sailors safely past the rocks and help avert shipping catastrophes. Not far from the lighthouse is Refviksand, said to be one of the best beaches in the country.

The southernmost point of the Norwegian mainland is Cape Lindesnes in the province of Vest-Agder. From the old lighthouse, popular with daytrippers, to the North Cape, where the European continent plunges abruptly into the ocean, it's exactly 2,518 kilometres (1,565 miles). There are then 1,300 kilometres (800-odd miles) of icy water before the Spitsbergen Islands, Europe's final outpost, valiantly emerge from the crashing waves.

The south of Norway consists of 16 provinces which house the majority of the population, the highest concentration being in and around Oslo with 450,000 inhabitants (80 per square kilometre). Almost as many again inhabit the city's green belt Akershus, the aptly-named "house of fields". Together with Ostføld along its southern boundaries Akershus is the undisputed granary of Norway where the land has been farmed for 10,000 years. Subsequently, no other part of the country is as rich in Stone Age relics and remains. In complete contrast the province of Telemark has only 2% of its area devoted to agriculture.

The Norway of the fjords begins in the province of Rogaland where in c. 855 Harald Fair-Hair declared himself the first king of all Norway and the Vikings set sail for America.

The further north you travel, the more impressive the scenery becomes, with deep fjords and mountain giants dominating the countryside. The provinces which play host to this fantastic natural spectacle are Hordaland, Sogn og Fjordane, Møre og Romsdal and Sør- and Nord-Trøndelag.

Above:
The palace in Oslo is still lived in by the royal family. Whereas the park and grounds are open to the public, the palace is for the family's private use only.

Right:
The royal military band doesn't just play at special state receptions; public band concerts are a regular occurrence in the Norwegian capital.

Page 30/31:
From afar the fortress of Akershus greets the ships sailing into the harbour at Oslo. Once a fierce stronghold, during the 17th century it was converted into a picturesque Renaissance palace and now houses the Norwegian Resistance Museum.

Left:
Karl Johans Gate is the buzzing main thoroughfare of Oslo with the city's greatest abundance of (expensive) shops, boutiques and cafés.

Below:
Among the more prestigious buildings on Karl Johans Gate are the National Theatre and the old university, pictured here.

Right and below:
For many visitors the
Oslofjord is their first
impression of Norway.
Locals treat it as a great
place to relax and
escape from the bustle
of the city.

Top right and bottom:
The Norwegians are fervent sailors, with no selfrespecting south coast resort without its yachting harbour. Here Oslo (top) and Sandefjord (bottom).

Centre right:
Norway does have sandy beaches but sunbathing on the rocks at Larvik also has acertain appeal.

Bottom left:
Henrik Ibsen, whose critical dramas caused a stir throughout Europe, in a photograph from c. 1900.

Below:
Among the main attractions of the National Gallery in Oslo are the paintings by Norway's Romantics and the Munch collection.

Centre right:
The literary works of Knut Hamsun were written against the fantastic natural backdrop of his native Nordland.

Top right:
Bjørnstjerne Bjørnson and Edvard Grieg. Bjørnson won a Nobel Prize and wrote the Norwegian national anthem; Grieg made

Berlin, November 5, 1892. The art society launches an exhibition devoted to the then 29-year-old Norwegian artist Edvard Munch. One week later it closes – to the boos of a shocked, disgusted public unable to cope with Munch's unorthodox style.

This scandal, to date one of the biggest in Germany's history of art, deeply upset Munch but also made him famous almost overnight. "They fail to comprehend that there may be some sense behind these impressions (...), that a room can be red or blue (...). They are not capable of realising that this is serious – they think it is humbug (...) or derangement", he reasons in reaction to the course of events.

One year later in 1893 Munch finished "The Scream", his most famous work. Today's visitors to Oslo's National Gallery will find the comment "Can only have been painted by a madman" scribbled onto the red clouds in pencil. It's believed the words were penned by the artist himself.

FROM CHEMIST TO PLAYWRIGHT

In 1906 Munch designed the set for Max Reinhard's production of Henrik Ibsen's "Ghosts" staged at the Kammerspiele in Berlin. Ibsen himself (1828–1906) first trained as a chemist before turning to the theatre. His

AND CO.

Norwegian music famous the world over and composed the incidental music to Bjørnson's play "Sigurd Jorsalfar", among other works.

Bottom right:
Edvard Grieg and his wife lived in their Troldhaugen villa for 22 years.

early works were written in the true spirit of the Romantic age, with later pieces turning more towards the realist social drama. The plots are governed by the inner self, with dialogue and not action the prevalent mode of communication. This makes Ibsen's plays no less exciting – on the contrary. Individual crises sparked off by the constraints and double standards of the state and the church predominate. In this vein "The Pillars of Society", "A Doll's House" and "Ghosts" are among Ibsen's most successful works – abroad. In Norway itself he was first denounced as a denigrator of his own country, only being heralded as the most genial chronicler of his day at a much later date.

THE INEXPLICABLE STATES OF THE SOUL

In 1890, when Munch notated his artist's manifesto deploring naturalism and upholding "mood painting" in a single night in St Cloud, his fellow countryman Knut Hamsun (1859–1952) had his famous article entitled "The Life of the Soul" printed in which he

declared his support for a genre of poetry which described "the inexplicable states of the soul". Like Ibsen psychology played a major role in the books of Hamsun. He consciously opposed Ibsen's critical realism, however, opting instead for a form of natural mysticism. He saw a chance for the future of society not in the uprooted dwellers of the cities but in the sons of the soil tilling the land out in the country. This at least seems to be the message in his 1917 novel "Growth of the Soil" which won him the Nobel Prize for Literature in 1920.

Incidentally, Hamsun was neither the first nor the last Norwegian to have this honour bestowed upon him. Bjørnstjerne Bjørnson (1832–1910), who during his lifetime was far more popular in Norway than Ibsen, was awarded the prize in 1903, followed by Sigrid Undset (1882–1949) in 1928.

NORDIC MUSIC – EDVARD GRIEG

In 1867 Ibsen published his fairytale drama "Peer Gynt" for which Edvard Grieg (1843–1907) wrote two orchestral suites of incidental music as the playwright requested. In his endeavour to create music which was essentially Nordic in style he wove elements of his native folklore into his compositions. Grieg claimed that he did not wish to build churches and temples like Bach and Beethoven but to create "places for people (...) where they can feel happy and at home". Judging by the number of visitors from near and far who flock to his home Villa Troldhaugen outside Bergen each summer, now a museum, it can be assumed that his intentions were successful.

Below:
Lindesnes fyr is not only the oldest but also the southernmost lighthouse in the country. From here it's a long 2,518 kilometres (1,565 miles) to the North Cape.

Left:
From 1905 until 1968 Sandefjord was home to much of the Norwegian whaling fleet who set out from here for the icy waters of the Arctic Ocean.

Page 44/45:
The Gloppefossen Falls
in Aust-Agder may not
be as imposing as
Norway's higher cascades
yet are none the less
spectacular or romantic.

Right:
The Prekestolen (Pulpit
Rock) shoots 600 metres
(ca. 1,970 feet) up from
the serene waters of the
Lysefjord. The breath-
taking view from the top
is the reward for two
hours' strenuous hiking
up the mountainside.

Top:
A picnic atop the pulpit
rock, with a sheer drop
on three sides, is not for
the faint-hearted.

Above:
Together with the North
Cape and the
Geirangerfjord, the
Prekestolen is one of
Norway's most popular
photographic motifs.

Right:
Although the entire quarter had to be rebuilt following the terrible fire of 1702, Bryggen, with its pointed gables and slatted facades, has lost none of its fascination for visitors. Where Hanseatic traders once lived and worked are now shops, restaurants and art galleries.

Norway's largest expanse of orchard can be found along the Hardangerfjord. Flowering meadows near Ringøy (left), reddening cherries against the backdrop of snowy mountain peaks and blossoming fruit trees near Lofthus (below and bottom) herald the glorious arrival of spring.

The most famous and fourth-largest waterfall in the country is Vøringfossen on the Hardangervidda plateau, made accessible to the public at the end of the 19th century.

If you go to Norway, one thing you'll be sure to see a lot of is water. Here the Låtefossen Falls in all their wild splendour.

Utne on the Folgefonn peninsula is beautifully situated on the shores of the Hardangerfjord and also has the oldest hotel in Norway.

The gaping steel jaws of the ferry linking Kvanndal to Utne.

A narrow pathway takes you under the Steindalsfossen Waterfall near Norheimsund on the western banks of the Hardangerfjord.

Below:
In Finse, the highest
railway station in
Norway, both the trains
and the dog sleighs seem
to be having problems
with the weather.

Right:
Winter has a firm grip
on the Hardangervidda
mountain plateau for
much of the year. The
pass built at the end of

the 1960s ensures that
cars can now access the
plateau all year round,
regardless of storms,
snow and ice

Above:
The Bergen railway, the
legendary stretch of
track running across the

Hardangervidda plateau
from Bergen to Oslo, was
opened in 1909.

54

The Sørfjord is part of the Hardangerfjord system, a narrow side arm stretching south to Odda.

The Hardangervidda on a warm summer's night, the time of year when the plateau is humming with nature lovers studying the seasonal multitude of flora and fauna. With a bit of luck they might even spot one of the reindeer living here in the wild.

Left:
*Norway's biggest glacier
is the Jostedalsbreen,
whose icy fingers cling to
the mountainside in
all directions.*

Below:
*With its snow-capped
peaks, Jotunheimen,
the "land of the giants",
is one of the highest
ranges of mountains
in Scandinavia.*

Above:
*The glacial world of the
Jostedalsbreen is an
intriguing place to
explore. Here curious
visitors study the ice at
Nigardsbreen at the end
of the Jostedal.*

Above:
*Not something you see
every day; a summer
solstice bonfire in deep
snow near Vossadalen
in Fjordland.*

Below:
*Nedstryn in Fjordland.
This charming village is
situated on the Nordfjord
which splits into three
tributaries inland.*

Top right:

Where the Aurlandsfjord ends, the Flåmdal begins. The main town of Flåm is where Norway's steepest railway line begins its precipitous climb up into the mountains.

Centre right:

The stave church at Undredal is the tiniest place of worship in Scandinavia, measuring under four metres (13 feet) in width.

Bottom right:

Riding a horse and trap to the Briksdalsbreen, one of the most beautiful glacial arms in the country, it's as if the clock has turned back 100 years.

Above:
This old farm in Uppland, the only province not to border on the sea, is an oasis of peace and quiet.

Right:
Lillehammer is not just worth visiting for the impressive Winter Olympics facilities alone. It also has the best and most interesting open-air museum in Norway, where examples of what is commonly known as "rose painting" are preserved.

Left:
At the De Sandvigske Samlinger Open-Air Museum its founder, dentist Anders Sandvig, has managed to save 150 buildings from decay. This storehouse is just one of them; others include farm-houses, grazing huts, schools and Garmo's ancient stave church.

Below left and right:
Children sporting floral wreaths for the mid-summer's eve festivities in Lillehammer. Scandinavians celebrate the summer solstice long and hard – and Norway is no exception.

63

Left:
*Norway's largest inland
lake, the Mjøsa, ends in
Lillehammer where the
Gudbrandstal begins,
one of the largest valleys
in the east which has
played a major part in
shaping regional history
and culture.*

Below:
*East of the old copper
mining town of Røros is
Lake Femund, Engerdal.
Local Sami have herded
reindeer on the shores of
the lake since the 16th
century.*

Above:
*The Rondane National
Park is divided between
the regions of Oppland
and Hedmark. The park
encompasses c. 600
square kilometres (230
square miles) of the high
mountain range
of the same name.*

Left page:
The Sognefjord, the
"king of the fjords", is
a place of superlatives;
it's the longest arm of
the sea to curl beneath
the highest mountains
in Norway and around
the largest continental
glacier in Europe.

The Næøyfjord gets very
narrow, with mountains
shooting 1,000 metres
(3,280 feet) up into the
sky on either side of you.

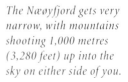

The Strynsvatnet –
a lake and not a fjord –
is 15 kilometres (9 miles)
long and not quite
200 metres (660 feet)
deep.

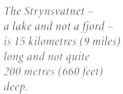

Page 68/69:
One of the most
photographed natural
spectacles in the country
is the Geirangerfjord,
seen here from the
viewing platform at
Flydalsjuvet.

The history of Norway's fjords begins in the Tertiary Period when the Scandinavian peninsula lifted and folded. In the glacial periods which followed the land disappeared under an enormous sheet of ice. This grew steadily, forging its way west from the mountains down into the valleys. The rocky bed of this giant glacial plane grew deeper and deeper, creating impressive U-shaped valleys. The ice not only cut down into the rock but also spread its huge weight out across this country in the making. The intense pressure on the earth's surface caused the land to become depressed. Inland, where the mass and also the load of the ice was much greater, the surface level dropped by several hundred metres.

THE SEA SNAKES INLAND

Following the last great ice age around 10,000 years ago the ice began to melt. The Atlantic Ocean rose and flooded the valleys, snaking inland to fill the jagged rents in the landscape. Norway's fjords were born.

Although very different in size, depth and form the fjords have several characteristics in common. Deposits of silt and scree are greatest

Left:
In Nordland the fjords are often rocky and narrow on the coast, such as here near Sandnessjoen.

Below:
The Aurlandsfjord splits off from the Sognefjord a long way inland.

Right:
View of the Saltfjord south of Bodø with its famous tidal current of the same name, one of the largest maelstroms in the world. This natural phenomenon, where vast quantities of water are forced through an extremely narrow channel, is most impressive at full and new moon.

THE FJORDS

Bottom right:
*Norway's sheltered fjords
are the ideal places to
erect oil rigs. One of the
largest to date is being
constructed here in the
Vatsfjord in Rogaland.*

at the beginnings and ends of the fjords where the water is shallowest. The middle section is all the deeper, with the Sognefjord plunging 1,308 metres (4,291 feet) down into the rock beneath its surface. At 200 kilometres (124 miles) it's also the longest fjord in the country. Superlatives like these are the result of mountain glaciers carving extensive waterways on their long route to the sea.

The best place to study the interplay of fjord and glacier is the Holandsfjord just beyond the Arctic Circle. The fjord has chiselled its way right up to the eternal ice of Norway's second-largest glacier, the Svartisen, which in turn lazily stretches a glacial arm, the Engabreen, towards the water.

ANCIENT WORKS OF ART

Speaking of water, its temperatures along

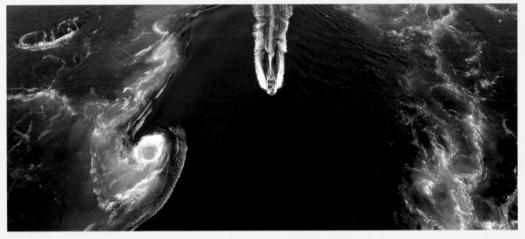

Norway's west coast are relatively high compared to those at similar degrees of latitude. This is due to the Gulf Stream which warms both land and sea, enabling the country to be inhabited right up into the wastes of the north. Ancient settlements going back 11,000 years have been discovered as far north as the Varangerfjord, with many of these prehistoric peoples carving incredible works of art into the rocks which provide us with vital clues as to their existence. Over 2,000 were discovered on the shores of the Altafjord to the west in 1973. They are estimated to be ca. 9,000 years old and are now a UNESCO World Heritage Site. The Altafjord also makes headlines for a very different reason; it is the most northerly region in the world where grain can still be cultivated.

People gradually began to conquer Norway via the fjords where the first communities were established. Finds show that the ancient settlers probably felt more comfortable on the water's edge than further into the land which must have risen up before them like an impenetrable wall of rock. The fjords provided them with both a source of nourishment and a fairway; our words "firth" and "ford" are derived from the Norwegian fjord. It is thus hardly surprising that the country's political history also began on a "fjord". In 997 Olav Tryggyvason founded a royal city on the Trondheimfjord which he named Nidaros. It was from here that the Vikings set out for America, centuries before Christopher Columbus. Ships bringing the first import back from Newfoundland – a cargo of wood – also docked at what is now Trondheim.

Considering how important the fjords were and still are for the population of Norway it almost goes without saying that the country's modern capital Oslo is also on the water – on a fjord.

The stave church at Lom in Uppland dates back to the 12th/13th century. Heads of dragons were attached to the roof to protect worshippers from evil spirits.

Left:

In Ringebu, one of the oldest trading centres in the Gudbrandsdal, stands an impressive example of a stave church. It was erected near a thingstead in c. 1200 and extended in the 17th century.

Below:

Despite its 17th-century refurbishment, the pillared interior of the church at Lom has managed to retain much of its original character. One of its particular gems is the ornate Baroque chancel.

With its eleven hairpin bends, the Trollstigen or Troll's Ladder south of Åndalsnes is one of the most spectacular mountain passes in Norway and an absolute must when you're in Fjordland.

Ålesund is just under 100 years old. After a raging fire in 1904 the town had to rebuilt; the houses around the inner harbour in particular have been remodelled in eloquent Art Nouveau.

Left:
This ancient fishing harbour in Otnes, Møre og Romsdal, seems to effuse Nordic tranquillity.

Below:
Molde has just over 20,000 inhabitants and is known locally as the "city of the rose". It also plays host to an international jazz festival each summer, set against the backdrop of the lush Romsdal alps.

Left:
Perhaps the most impressive features of Nidaros Cathedral are its proportions – 102 metres (335 feet) long and 50 metres (164 feet) wide – and the light flooding in through Gabriel Kielland's stained glass windows.

Below:
Trondheim may still have many of its delightful wooden houses and look back on 1,000 years of history, yet with its university, research institutes, museums and lively shopping arcades it's very much a modern city.

Below centre:
So that cycling up Trondheim's hills isn't too strenuous, there's a special bike lift installed on this steep slope.

Above:
One of the highlights of Trondheim's old town centre is the wooden bridge (Bybrua) over the Nidelva framing colourful riverside warehouses.

Below:
In Røros, where copper was once mined, much of the old settlement has been preserved. The miners' simple crofts and the less humble residences of the mine's directors were made of wood, with only the village church erected in stone.

Right:
Evening sky over the Trondheimfjord which winds its way inland towards the northeast.

Above:
River Størdalselv in the province of Nord-Trøndelag is famous for its salmon and trout.

FISHERMEN AND

There was once nothing Norway's fishermen feared more than the "black years" of the trade, when potentially lucrative shoals of fish shunned native waters. Crises such as these were, however, relatively infrequent and soon blew over. That has now all changed. Getting a good haul nowadays is a once-in-a-blue-moon occurrence; much of what has been left in the North Sea amounts to little more than small fry.

THE PERFECTION OF FISHING TECHNOLOGY

This is a trend which has been observed over the course of several decades; the reasons for this drastic development are thus not new. One of the major causes for the decimation of the fish population is the constant striving to perfect modern machinery. Motor boats have a much larger range than craft which rely on wind or muscle power to transport them across the water. The introduction of the fish-finding echo sounder has also ensured

that the prey have little chance of escaping their pursuers. In 1880 there was a bloody battle in the Trollfjord between crews manning what were then state-of-the-art steamers and locals struggling to make a living in their tiny, traditional fishing boats. Technological advance has bulldozed fishing well into the 21st century since then but, unlike in 1880, not necessarily to its advantage. Contemporary trawlers can now net such large quantities that the fish population is not able to regenerate fast enough to satisfy demand. Modern machinery has managed to put itself out of business.

Left:
An entire museum has been devoted to the salmon at Lærdalsøyri, a small community huddled at the mouth of River Lærdalselva, Norway's prime venue for salmon fishing.

Below:
Fishermen from the Lofoten Islands out cod fishing, an occupation which is becoming increasingly frustrating as the shoals diminish.

Far right:
Hundreds of fishing boats head out to sea between the middle of January and the middle of April when cod come to the islands to spawn.

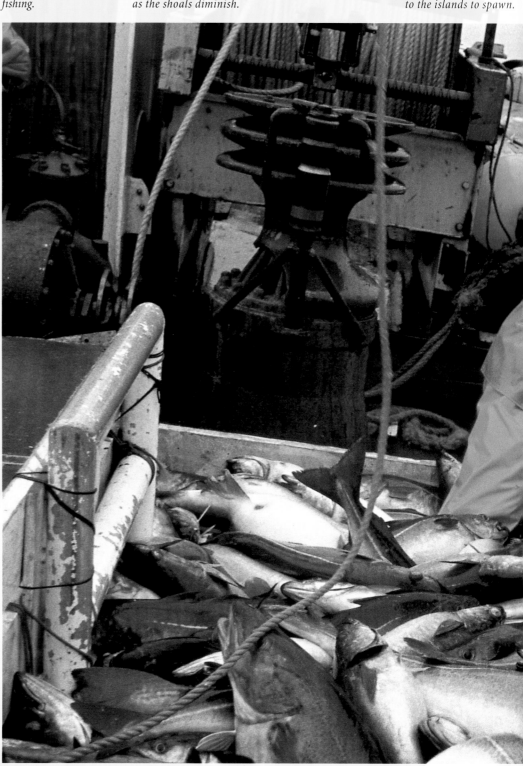

FISH FARMERS

THE ENDANGERED CAPELIN

Centre right:
Gutting fish – here in Henningsvær on the Lofoten Islands – is not a pleasant job.

Bottom right:
Very occasionally you might see cod left outside to dry on wooden racks.

Whereas in the past it was claimed that "only" a few popular varieties of fish, such as the herring and the cod, were in danger, today nobody can deny that the entire ecological system of the North Sea is in peril. The capelin (Mallotus villosus), a species of smelt from the salmon family, is a good example of how a little tampering with nature can result in grave consequences. Of no great use to man, the capelin is a great delicacy for the cod who, now that the North Sea is practically devoid of its prime source of nourishment, has abandoned terrestrial waters in favour of the Barents Sea where capelin can still be found.

ALTERNATIVE AQUACULTURE?

The beginning of the 1970s marked the advent of a possible alternative to conventional fishing: aquaculture. Floating cages were submerged in Norway's fjords for the breeding of salmon and rainbow trout by fishermen turned fish farmers. The cages were designed to keep the migrating salmon in one place and to provide it with the food it needed to give it its characteristic pink tinge in captivity. The downside of any kind of intensive livestock farming – aquaculture being no exception – is that there is a high risk of pests and diseases destroying the stock. The biggest problem facing fish farmers, however, has proved to be algae which thrive on the warming and pollution of the water, increasing as the fish stocks decrease. Plagued by algae, fish farmers can only move their cages to a less endangered spot and hope for the best.

Like fishing itself, fish processing has also undergone radical change. The great age of the Norwegian fish canning industry based in Stavanger, which unashamedly exploited both women and children, came to an end before the Second World War. Women were also put to work processing dried fish, for many years the country's major export. Norway's particular speciality was dried, salted cod. In summer the catch was laid out to dry on the rocky cliffs and frequently turned to stop it rotting or burning. If the weather held, the fish was ready for export within the month and was shipped out to all corners of the globe from Kristiansund, the centre of production.

Dried fish is still manufactured today but usually now prepared in heated sheds. If you're very lucky you might still see fish drying on the wooden racks which were long part of Norway's fishing tradition.

The Varangerfjord in Finnmark differs from the other fjords in that it juts inland from the east. The little hamlet of Vestre Jakobselv clutches its northern shores.

or several years the geographical centre of Norway has had a new focal point in the Tosen Tunnel which links the trading town of Brønnøysund with the E6 highway. Here Norway's administrative structure emulates the topography dictated by nature. Just south of the tunnel the province of Nordland begins, the second-largest region in Norway with just under a quarter of a million inhabitants. A third of these live on the many islands offshore – particularly the Lofotens and Vesterålens. There are only two proper cities in Nordland: Narvik, the largest loading harbour in the world thanks to the abundance of iron ore brought here from Kiruna in Sweden, and Bodø, home to the military's supreme command for northern Norway's air force and navy and also Northern Europe's NATO headquarters.

Nordland runs into the province of Troms whose regional capital Tromsø is also known as the "gateway to the Arctic". This is where the great polar explorers Amundsen, Nansen and Andrèe set off on their intrepid expeditions. Today around 50,000 people inhabit the town. Many come here from the smaller towns and villages in the area to find work and entertainment. For with its over 50 restaurants, bars, night clubs and even its own brewery, Tromsø is also known locally as the "Paris of the north".

Leaving the bright lights of Tromsø twinkling in the distance the solitary wastes of the north begin. Finnmark is both the largest and most sparsely populated province in the country. Although gas and oil have been found off the coast, the few people who manage to survive up here feel neglected by Oslo, almost like the Siberians of Norway; Finnmark was also once a place of correction and exile for state criminals.

Below:

On the bridge of the
Narvik full concentration
is called for when
turning the boat in the
narrow fjords.

Below:

A trip along the legendary
Norwegian Hurtigrute
from Bergen to Kirkenes
and back delivers what
all the adverts promise;
it really is one of the
"most beautiful sea
journeys in the world".

Right:

One of the major appeals
of the Hurtigrute, which
has been trawling the
coastal resorts since
1893, is the magnificent
scenery which seems to
change at every turn.

Above:

The high point of any
Hurtigrute journey are
the entrance and turning
manoeuvres in the
narrow Trollfjord when
the men at the helm
demonstrate their skill.

Above:

As the ships almost never
lose sight of land and
weigh anchor over
30 times during the trip,
there are plenty of
chances to get in some
shore leave.

Page 88/89:
Sun, sea and swirling mist in a midnight photo of the coast near Grimstad in Nordland, *once home to Norway's two most famous writers, Knut Hamsun and Henrik Ibsen.*

Below:
Narvik was the scene of ferocious fighting between the Germans and the Allies during the Second World War. Almost completely oblit- *erated, the present town, set against a fantastic mountain panorama, is the product of frenetic post-war building activity.*

Top right:
March is still very much a winter month in Nordland. Here, a snowplough trying to clear the E6.

Centre right:
This monument marks the spot where motorists travelling north on the E6 enter the Arctic Circle.

Bottom right:
What will the archaeologists of the future make of the strange graffiti sprayed onto this rock in Narvik?

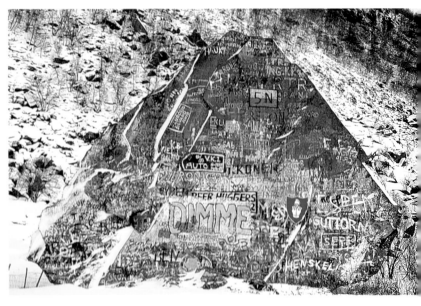

Page 92/93:
A wintry evening in Mosjøen on the Vefsnfjord: Nordland in snow.

Right and below:
Winter in Norway is long and harsh. Whereas its human inhabitants primarily suffer from too many hours of darkness, the chief concern of the country's animals – here an elk – is where to find food.

Narvik	352
Fauske	100
Rognan	69

Above:
*Snow, snow and more
snow, here piled up
along the E6 on the
Arctic Circle. In these
conditions it's best to
drive with studded tyres.*

Left:
*Once cut off from the out-
side world in the winter,
the lonely farms so
typical of the Norwegian
landscape are now
accessible by road all
year round.*

Below:
Norway's scenery is not only dramatic but also extremely versatile. One thing it doesn't lack, however, is water in its many different guises; here in emerald green at the ferry port in Skutvik.

Top right:
Beyond the Arctic Circle
the vegetation has to
adapt to survive. Trees
here grow on a slant.

Centre right:
The Brønnøysund in
Nordland is a majestic
stretch of water.

Bottom right:
Despite the extreme
climate in Nordland
settlement here goes back
to the Stone Age, as these
rock carvings illustrate.

The fishing village of
Eggum on the Lofotens
basking in the eerie light
of the midnight sun,
which changes every-
thing from sky colour
to air temperature
to human temperament.

*Reine on Moskenesøy in
the Lofotens is a modest
fishing community on
the Kirkefjord, very*

*close to the village
which has the shortest
name in the world: Å.*

Left:
*Even if the grand era of
Lofotens fishing is over,
fish are still very much
a composite part of
its life and landscape.
Henningsvær, spread
between several small
islands, is just one of
the places where fishing
still takes on a
traditional guise.*

Top:
*A fleet of cutters out
fishing for young Arctic
cod near Henningsvær,
who come to the Lofotens
to spawn between
January and April.*

Above:
*The traditional method
of drying cod is on out-
door racks made of
wood. In its dried state
cod was long a major
Norwegian export.*

Page 102/103:
*Fresh cod is still dried
according to tradition
near Andenes in the
Vesterälen Islands, just
north of the Lofotens.*

Left:
Ramberg has a wonderful half-moon sandy beach, flat enough even for bikes (although you won't get very far heading out to sea!)

Below:
The morning light of the north begins to shimmer on the water and mountains of the Selfjord.

Top right:
The Hurtigrute Museum in Stokmarknes takes a retrospective look at the early days of the legendary coastal ferry.

Lynx's paw" is the name the locals have given the archipelago off the west coast of Norway, a collection of four large North Sea islands surrounded by smaller islets. The abundant waters of the Lofoten Islands were legendary in the early Middle Ages, attracting settlers to the islands to fish the plentiful shoals of cod. Communities flourished, with Kabelvåg – now just a small village – blossoming into the Nordland centre of trade under King Håkon IV. Each year between January and April cod flocked to the shores to spawn where they were awaited by scores of fishermen from all over the country, nets at the ready. 20,000 still worked the islands after the Second World War, fuelling the rumour that the fish here would last until eternity.

SLEEPING IN SHIFTS

It hit hard when people realised that such prognoses were unfounded. Where once 50 million kilograms (110 million pounds) of fish were hauled from the sea, today not even half this amount is trawled. Many of the inhabitants had to start thinking about an alternative source of income. Their houses, which in their heyday had seen three to four shifts of fishermen sharing beds which never grew cold, began to fall into disrepair. And then came the

tourists, first holidaymaking Norwegians and then visitors from further afield. Dilapidated fishing huts, "rorbuer", were turned into idyllic holiday cottages to accommodate the sudden multitude of paying guests. Some of these ancient wooden cabins still exist in their original guise, such as in Nusfjord on Flakstadøy, for example, the smallest of the four main islands. The long sandy beaches here are also not too crowded in summer as the island is – still – without a hotel.

THE LOFOTENS

Centre and bottom right: On Vestvagøy Island near Borg archaeologists have excavated the remains of a Viking villa which is now on display at the Viking Museum in Lofotr. People dressed in Viking costume demonstrate to visitors what life during the Viking period was like.

MAELSTROMS AND TROLLS

Nearby Moskenesøy is the most southerly of the islands – which doesn't necessarily mean it's spared the wild storms which rage here throughout the winter months. Its mountains ward off the worst of the weather, sheltering its more northerly neighbours. There are other dangers, however. Between the southernmost point of Moskenesøy and the tiny islet of Mosken lurks a swirling maelstrom which devours not only people – as Edgar Allan Poe and Jules Verne have so vividly described – but anything unlucky enough to become ensnared in its angry current. Despite its obvious hazards the maelstrom is an impressive natural phenomenon, its waters bubbling and churning as if heated

by an underwater furnace. The powerful spectacle is caused by the sea being forced into the Vestefjord at a speed of 12 kilometres (seven miles) an hour through a narrow channel just four kilometres (two-and-a-half miles) long, with a difference of four metres (13 feet) in height to overcome.

For those who prefer to face danger from a safer distance the Trollfjord is guaranteed to take your breath away. It cuts along the most northerly island of the group, Austvågøy, which also has the administrative centre of the Lofotens in Svolvær. At 200 metres (656 feet) wide the Trollfjord is not only the narrowest of Norway's magnificent waterways; it's also squeezed into a spectacularly perpendicular corset of rock. For descendants of the Vikings, as the captains steering boatloads of tourists through the fjord like to see themselves, manoeuvring in a space as tight as this is absolutely no problem, however. Danger threatens here in a very different form – if you believe the legend. As the name suggests,

the fjord has a namesake, a wicked troll more dangerous and terrible than all of the Lofoten's maelstroms and winter storms put together. You have been warned...

Vestvågøy is not only the largest of the islands but also the flattest. Most visitors first set foot on the Lofoten Islands here in Stamsund. After admiring the sheer precipice of the Lofotenveggen or Lofoten Wall shooting up into the heavens from the sea, once ashore it can be explored in detail – knowing that if it's Norway's scenic superlatives you've come for, you won't be disappointed.

Surrounded by water
and mountain peaks, the
historical monument
and fishing community
of Nusfjord is possibly
one of the most scenic
spots in the Lofotens.

Right:
Land merges with the
sea near Vonheim on the
island of Vestvagøy. For
many centuries the sea
wasn't just a source of
nourishment but also the
only way of reaching the
neighbouring islands
before the present roads
and bridges were built.

Above:
Sun and shade paint
fantastic patterns on the
hills of the Lofotens,
constantly altering the
shape and mood of the
islands.

Right:
Near Eggum on
Vestvagøy Island, a tiny
village in the northwest.
Unusually the lake here
is not full of saltwater
but freshwater.

Left:
Hamnøy is one of the old fishing ports on the Lofotens which weave along the east coast like a string of pearls, protected from the elements by lofty mountains.

Top left:
The minute church of
Sildpollen on the Lofoten
Islands seems lost
against the expansive
backcloth of sea and
mountains.

Centre left:
The men of Andenes
still hunt down whales
like their ancestors
before them – thankfully
no longer to kill them
but to show them off to
admiring visitors.

Bottom left:
Taking a dip in the
Altafjord in Finnmark
where Stone Age settlers
once enjoyed the
relatively mild climate.

Right:
The Polar Museum in Tromsø explains why the commune was so important as the gateway to the Arctic Ocean. In the reconstructed Svalbard hut you can get a taste of everyday life on Spitsbergen Island.

Below:
Tromsø's major landmarks are its extremely high bridge, linking the old town island of Tromsøy to the mainland, and the Arctic Cathedral (Tromsdalen Kirke) with its symbolic architecture.

Top left:
*Kautokeino is both the
largest and the least
populated community in
Norway. Its nickname
"reindeer city" alludes to
the fact that one third*

*of the inhabitants are
in the reindeer trade.
One of the town's great
attractions are the
reindeer sledge races
at Easter.*

Bottom left:
*At the Easter service
in Kautokeino the Sami
wear traditional
costume.*

Below:
*Kautokeino is also the
Sami centre of Norway.
The bright attire worn
by the natives of the
north is usually only
donned on special feast
days.*

*Page 116/117:
The atmospheric light
of the midnight sun
over Stabbursdalen
in Finnmark.*

115

Right:
The river forging its way
through the Alta Gorge is
thought to be one of the
best places for salmon
fishing in the world.

Below:
The River Teno east of
the Alta Gorge is also
popular with anglers.
Its far bank is part
of Finland.

Above:
Bridges like this one near
Skaidi are no seldom
occurrence in the wild-
mark and in many places
the only way of crossing
a river without getting
your feet wet.

Left:
Where man has to
dangerously negotiate
the wild rapids in a boat,
salmon simply leap.

Page 120/121:
The final destination on
a long journey; the
North Cape, bathed in the
magical light of the mid-
night sun, is the most
famous cliff in Europe.

A brief lesson in geography as seen from the Norwegian perspective. According to these Narvik signposts it's about 2,000 kilometres (1,240 miles) to Hamburg and twice that to Rome. The distances given for within Norway don't seem to tarry; the inland traveller has to cover a comparatively staggering 1,500 kilometres (930 miles) from Narvik to Oslo and over 1,000 (620) to Kirkenes. Help, anyone?

Credits

Design
hoyerdesign grafik gmbh, Freiburg

Map
Fischer Kartografie, Fürstenfeldbruck

Translation
Ruth Chitty, Schweppenhausen

Printed in Germany
Repro by Artilitho, Trento, Italy
Printed by Konkordia GmbH, Bühl
Bound by Josef Spinner Großbuchbinderei GmbH, Ottersweier
© 2002 Verlagshaus Würzburg GmbH & Co. KG
© Photos: Max Galli, St. Moritz, Switzerland

ISBN 3-8003-1589-0